Navigation

Navigation

Poems by

Linda Neal Reising

© 2025 Linda Neal Reising. All rights reserved.
This material may not be reproduced in any form, published,
reprinted, recorded, performed, broadcast,
rewritten or redistributed without
the explicit permission of Linda Neal Reising.
All such actions are strictly prohibited by law.

Cover design by Shay Culligan
Cover image by Catrin Welz-Stein
Author photo by Heather Thompson Morlan

ISBN: 978-1-63980-690-4

Kelsay Books
502 South 1040 East, A-119
American Fork, Utah 84003
Kelsaybooks.com

Acknowledgments

Thank you to the following publications, in which versions of these poems previously appeared:

Beyond Words Magazine: "Chambers of the Heart"
Broad River Review: "Horsman"
Comstock Review: "After Learning That a Woman and Her Baby Were Killed in a Bombing of a Ukrainian Maternity Hospital," "From the Kitchen Window: Sunday Morning, Early June"
eMerge: "Illumination," "This Is Not a Symbolic Poem About Cicadas"
The Heartland Review: "What You Missed While You Were in Grandma's Living Room with All the Other Women"
Indiana Humanities: "The Reason We Gather for the Solar Eclipse"
Let Me Say This: A Dolly Parton Poetry Anthology (Madville Press): "Dolly's Debut"
Nimrod: "Navigation"
Perpetual Astonishment (Beyond Words Press): "After Learning That a Woman and Her Baby Were Killed in the Bombing of a Ukrainian Maternity Hospital," "Bugs in Amber," "Chambers of the Heart," "Disappeared," "Dolly's Debut," "Earth Day Lockdown," "Education of a Sixth-Generation Cherokee Refugee," "Even in Oklahoma," "From the Kitchen Window: Sunday, Early June," "Grand Lake O' the Cherokees," "Illumination," "Made in America," "Perpetual Astonishment," "The Hands She Was Dealt," "What You Missed While You Were in Grandma's Living Room with All the Other Women"
Red Penguin Books: "Soon"

So It Goes (The Kurt Vonnegut Library and Museum): "Claude," "Earth Day Lockdown," "Education of a Sixth-Generation Cherokee Refugee," "Johnny Keene," "Perpetual Astonishment," "POW"

The Working Man's Hand: Celebrating Woody Guthrie—Poems of Protest and Resistance 2023: "Made in America," "The Hands She Was Dealt"

Contents

Navigation   17

PART I

After Learning That a Woman and Her Baby Were
   Killed in the Bombing of a Ukrainian
   Maternity Hospital   21
From the Kitchen Window:
   Sunday Morning, Early June   22
Perpetual Astonishment   23
Earth Day Lockdown   24
This Is Not a Symbolic Poem About Cicadas   25
Toy Time   26
Bugs in Amber   27
Enter Autumn   28
Valentine's Day   29
Vibrations   30
Benediction   31
Soon   32

PART II

Illumination   35
Dolly's Debut   36
What You Missed While You Were in Grandma's
   Living Room with All the Other Women   37
Partial Eclipse   39
1970   40
Unchained Melody   41
Shangri-La   42
Motown Comes to Notown   43
Ode to the Gray Greaser   44
Persephone's Seduction   45
Outside the Snak Shak—1972   46
If Life Were a Rom-Com   47

PART III

Education of a Sixth-Generation Cherokee Refugee	51
Even in Oklahoma	53
The Land of Milk and Honey	54
Uncle Rocky	56
Grand Lake O' the Cherokees	57
Saturday Night Refuge	58
Made in America	59
The Hands She Was Dealt	60
My Mother Said Nothing	61
Johnny Keene	62
When PBS Came to Picher, Oklahoma	63
Remembering Oklahoma	65

PART IV

Chambers of the Heart	69
Trespassers	70
The Reason We Gather for the Solar Eclipse	71
Mesa Verde	73
POW	75
Claude	76
Horsman	78
Disappeared	80
The Poetry of Their Names	82
Medicare Physical	83
An Apology to My Father	84
Dreams Deferred	86

This book is dedicated to all of the teachers—professional and otherwise—who have helped me navigate through life, and to all of the editors who have given my poems safe harbor.

Navigation

I've read that there are many poems
in circulation today,

and I picture them
in their little paper boats,
sailing through sixty thousand miles
of blood vessels—twice around
the equator—floating on two thousand
gallons of blood, bouncing on waves
at each heartbeat—three billion
in an average life—

and I'm sure some are elegies
written for the eight million
blood cells dying every second,
and some are odes, praising their rebirth,
and some are free verse, wheeling
their way along at full speed, twenty
seconds to circumnavigate the whole body,
until they float into port, pulling up to dock
beside their friends—newspapers, coins,
and a few soggy library books.

PART I

*The goal of life is to make your heartbeat
match the beat of the universe,
to match your nature with Nature.*
—Joseph Campbell

After Learning That a Woman and Her Baby Were Killed in the Bombing of a Ukrainian Maternity Hospital

Each spring a cardinal resurrects
her nest in the spirea bush outside
our library window. Patient
in her pursuits, she scavenges
wheat straws from fallow fields,
dried pine needles, tiny twigs.
The cupped cradle, perched
on forked branches, clings
there, awaiting the clutch
of eggs to come, the soft songs
she will croon as she broods.
But this morning, inside a flower bed,
just beginning to fill with green spears
of daffodils, her remains—feathers
so pale a red they verge on pink,
color of water tinged with blood.
We have heard the owl each night
claiming this territory, the same old story
of the strong taking what they want,
and now he has left behind nothing
but pinions, as if some tiny angel
tumbled to earth, slipped off her wings,
and chose to walk all the way back
to heaven.

From the Kitchen Window:
Sunday Morning, Early June

The ancient catalpa, brought down by wind
and whining blade years ago, has been reborn

from the inside, sporting two slender feminine
legs for trunk, now tossing blossoms, ruffled

and white like a young girl's church-day anklets.
A choir of day lilies gather around, opening

their throats in praise, shouting orange hallelujahs.
Nearby, mulberry trees have strewn their alms—

amethysts, garnets—onto the back patio,
luring the return of a young buck—all knees,

tail twitch, ear flick. Antlers that had been velvet
knobs a week ago have now grown stems,

promise of staghood, a time of bravado bellows
and earth pawing, locking rival horns to rule

as sultan of the harem. But this morning,
he gently bows his head, accepts each berry

with quivering lips, a solemn communion.
These are what the world needs on this Sunday

morning in June, a promise of resurrection,
an act of unbridled joy, a reminder of tender mercies.

Perpetual Astonishment

> *I belong to an unholy disorder—*
> *We call ourselves 'our Lady of*
> *Perpetual Astonishment.'*
> —Kurt Vonnegut, *A Man Without a Country*

Perhaps there is something holy, after all,
in this unholy disorder around us. Note
the spider, blood as blue as the Virgin's
robe, building a cathedral of orb webs.
Or the honeybee, sipping communion
from the Rose of Sharon, hovering
member of an angel host, its wings
practicing ascension as they beat
two hundred times per second.
Listen to an exaltation of larks
or watch an order of starlings
in their shiny cassocks, chanting
in notes too high for humans to hear.
Congregate among the Douglas
fir or the cedars, Biblical in size,
and know they confess in tongues
known only to them, seek redemption.
Look up into the vault of the night sky
where stars sing their own requiem,
and when they die, scatter their cores
into space, seeds for a new generation.
Let us all kneel at this altar, learn
the lessons of the supernova, to pass
along the amazement of this world,
to never forget to worship at the grotto
of Our Lady of Perpetual Astonishment.

Earth Day Lockdown

Maybe this is the way it will be.

Bearded mountain goats with shaggy
bellies and French horn horns
clapping their hooves across sidewalks
in Wales as they stroll past
a quaint store named "Ewe Felty Thing,"
while a cartoon sheep, tangled
in yarn, gapes from a window sign.

Or jackals, their canine noses
to the ground as they romp
in a park outside Tel Aviv,
sunning their coats, licking
their paws, as they wait
for night to fall, when they raise
their faces to the moon, howl triumph.

Or raccoons strolling empty paths
in Central Park. Deer using pedestrian
crossings in Japan. Wild boar
grazing rose gardens in Corsica.
Herds of buffalo striding through New
Delhi roads. Wild turkeys strutting
the suburbs of Baton Rouge. Coyotes
playing outside Dodger Stadium,
sightseeing the Golden Gate Bridge.
Ducks runway walking the Vegas Strip.

Maybe this is the way it will be
when we are gone for good.

This Is Not a Symbolic Poem About Cicadas

A twice poet laureate proclaims that *cicada*
is a word that writers should never use,
the mere sight of it bringing him up short,
causing him to classify it as cliché—trite
symbol of memory, transformation, rebirth.

But just this afternoon, when I stepped outside,
I, too, was brought up short by cicadas, clicking,
reverberating from their masculine membranes
on their ribbed abs and obliques. These dog-day
choir members, chanting congregational songs,

synchronize their voices, as they bask in glow
of late summer sunshine, send out courting
calls. Just like in a rock band, the drummer
with his wicked sticks always gets the girl,
so these guys resonate their hollow tymbal,

sometimes as much as four hundred eighty
times a second, and girl bugs perched on limbs
of willows and redbuds, play hard to get, feign
disinterest, as they sip sap with straw-like mouths,
waiting patiently, after seventeen years, for Mr. Right.

Toy Time

A study recently published in Animal Behavior suggests that bumblebees, when given a chance, like to fool around with toys.
—NPR

And now, even the bees, known for their buzzing
busyness, have decided a four-day work week,
a little "me" bee time, is needed. Researchers
in London have found that bees, bumbling
their way through a pathway leading to a feeding
area, will stop, hover mid-flight to contemplate
a detour, the proverbial diverging road of Frost
fame, offering new possibility. They question
their quest for pollination, their unflappable
faithfulness to their Queen, and head toward
a honey pot of hedonism. Clad in their rugby shirts
of black and gold, they enter a special arena,
a chamber with a smattering of small wooden balls—
balls to be rolled, somersaulted over in apian acrobatics,
danced backward in an unnatural bumblebee ballet.
They find for the first time what it is like to at last
stop to smell the roses, instead of spending each
of their waking hours stopping to smell the roses.

Bugs in Amber

> *All time is all time. It does not change . . .*
> *and you will find that we are all . . .*
> *bugs in amber.*
> —Kurt Vonnegut, Slaughterhouse-Five

Fifteen days after Kurt caught
his first breath of Indiana air,
Howard Carter felt the cold
exhale as he opened the burial
plot of the Boy King. In this place
known for riddles, he viewed
the *wonderful things* tucked
within Tut's tomb, hidden away
for three thousand revolutions
around the sun. Within the walls
of gypsum plaster, painted yellow,
lay gold amulets, bracelets, collars,
rings. And among the trove,
a treasure surprise—trade beads
from Europe and sculpted scarabs
carved from foreign amber, seeped
from trees, capturing within rosin's
sweetness, an insect, intact. Startled
to find it could not lift a foot,
unfold a wing, the captive surrendered
to sap, which hardened with time,
until the amber locked the creature
inside its own golden tomb, preserved,
as if time meant nothing, as if its chirring
had never ceased, and like all of us,
there was no reason for his being
here, except for chance, happenstance.

Enter Autumn

Enter autumn—cattails, gossiping
in clusters along the banks of the waterway, let loose
their cottony breath, floating whispered tufts
of fluff. Knobby milkweed pods, skin bronzed
with age, burst open, late-in-life birthing of flaxen-
haired seeds—snowy as egret plumes. They set sail,
drift on seasoned breezes, alight on rain-soft shores.
Once tame tomatoes, sunning alongside a brick
wall, discover themselves mummified, leaves and flesh
shriveled, entombed by cold, except for one perfect ruby
pendant that dangles in defiance like an embalmed
king's bounty. Nearby, a flock of migrant mourners
rise from a fallow field once ripened with wheat,
fall into formation, write a line of twilight lament.

Valentine's Day

The red-winged blackbirds have come back,
wearing hearts on their sleeves.
All week the pines have chanted atonements,
grackles and starlings begging forgiveness
for returning too soon. Even the moon,
ancient romantic, has been eclipsed
by Earth, an old lover we thought
we knew, could trust, but has thrust
us into this year without winter.
If the time comes when the reasoning
of seasons has been up-ended forever,
what will happen to our metaphors?
For now, we can only wait and watch
the murmuration of sparrows,
oscillating waves of winged
harbingers, sky writing in cursive
a lovelorn letter addressed
to all of us.

Vibrations

According to quantum physics, a particle vibrating due to your sound when you speak, can affect a molecule inside a star at the edge of the Universe instantly.
—Neil deGrasse Tyson

Let us speak softly, choose each word
with the same care given a robin's egg—
blue as a distant planet, a rare moon.
Think of the power our throats hold,
to send a tremor as far as a star, a star
whose light has seen a hundred years
of our nights. Let us mind what slips
from our lips in times when our minds
flare with molten rage. Who knows
what cosmic quaking might occur,
what celestial oscillation? An utterance,
even one as innocent as a cross mutter,
might create a supernova, luminous
star explosion. Just think of the tumult
caused by each scream, every cry. Instead,
let us chant ethereal odes to the vast Cosmos—
sing out Irish ballads, sacred psalms,
childhood lullabies.

Benediction

When dogs howl at 2 A.M.
they are answering the chant
of their monastic brethren, gathered
together with arrowed shoulder
blades as they send up lauds to Goddess
Moon. Or perhaps they long to join
the rowdy congregation, pawing dusty
earth around a hollow hickory log,
where quivering prey, prays, waiting
wide-eyed and unblinking. Maybe
the dogs sing a requiem to the stars
pasted onto velvet backdrop sky,
mourning an ancient time when they,
too, were free to roam, before campfire
wooed them close enough to lose
both ferocity and fear. It is that time
of early morning, Benediction hours,
when dogs sometimes remember
their sin against nature, throw back
their heads, intoning forgiveness.

Soon

Even the red fox and two half-grown
kits who lawn-lounged or pounced
the neighbor's zinnias all summer
have faded into the nearby fields
where cornstalks wear brown fatigues.
The last ruby tomatoes dangle from tangled
pendants. Porch geraniums have grown
Pre-Raphaelite necks.
Soon—maples will turn nutmeg, cinnamon.
Soon—the mourning calls of weary geese
      will chime morning.
Soon—the days will pull their shutters early.
Soon—cattails will exhale cotton breaths,
      a melancholy sighing, sighing.

PART II

The turning point in the process of growing up is when you discover the core of strength within you that survives all hurt.
—Max Lerner

Illumination

Summer evenings ablaze with fireflies,
lightning lanterns signaling in dew-tipped
grass, we paraded our bare, rock-toughened
feet up and down the mound of earth covering
the storm cellar—brides or queens in procession.
Then, in the distance, we would hear the whistle,
track clatter of a passenger train imagining
its way to a city, no stop near this one-stop-
light town, shuttered when Route 66 shuddered
to sleep. Inside the cars, silhouettes of diners,
profiles behind drawn shades, a beacon
on each table, a tableau of elegance dreamed
in our pretend, pre-teen world. And sometimes,
at the very end, a uniformed man stood holding
the railing of the caboose, raising his hand
in one swift wave or salute, as we cheered
this promise of leaving, peered down the track
until there was nothing left but a light so small,
it could have been just another firefly after all.

Dolly's Debut

My mother would pop the corn we had grown
in the garden, reward for our summer thumbs,
sore after shelling, separating pearl-like kernels
from cob. Daddy would bring home a six pack
of Grapette, glass bottles rattling inside
the cardboard carrier. These nights, we splurged,
split two bottles four ways, then clustered
around the television set, a nearly-new Zenith
color console, Christmas surprise my parents
paid out on time. That September Tuesday night,
we were prepping for the Porter Wagoner Show,
my father's favorite, although he still mourned
the leaving of Norma Jean, as if she were dead
instead of quitting to marry. At twelve, I rolled
my eyes at Speck Rhodes, the Wagonmasters,
the corny barn backdrop, the flashy suits,
the pompadours. But that night in '67,
when Porter introduced the "little gal" named
Dolly Parton, clad in her sleeveless red dress
with garnet brooch, sporting a platinum bouffant,
I sat up straight as she flashed her dimples
and began to wail "Dumb Blonde." Still buck-toothed,
pudgy, my braids as lifeless as sunning black snakes,
I dreamt of being her, believed that a plain
girl from the Ozark foothills could be re-made
into a star, a nova, if only she believed.

What You Missed While You Were in Grandma's Living Room with All the Other Women

Aunt Sandra taught us younger girls
how to pin up our hair with Dippity-Do,
sit under the dryer with its Jiffy Pop
bonnet, how to spit curl frames
around our foreheads ala Liz Taylor.

Aunt Sandra showed us how to load
a man's razor with double-edged blade,
to lather legs with a bar of Ivory,
then move furrows of foam, leaving
a flesh mirror of calves and thighs.

Aunt Sandra demonstrated how to stuff
the cups of our dime store bras, creating
Kleenex cleavage, how to step inside
a stiff standing cancan, wiggling
it up under an American Bandstand skirt.

Aunt Sandra taught us how to polish
our canvas tennis shoes with roll-on
white, to make our Keds look new again.
To match them with a plastic belt, cinched
to create curves we did not have yet.

Aunt Sandra directed us to form a line,
while she dropped the needle on the 45,
taught us to dance the Stroll, to weave
our feet in overlapping figure eights
to the smooth crooning of the Diamonds.

Aunt Sandra showed us how to hold
a Chesterfield between fingers, to flick,
to leave a strawberry red kiss print
on the filter, to turn a dimpled cheek
away to blow smoke through a pout.

Aunt Sandra dabbed perfume behind
our ears, turning the curvy cobalt bottle
over and over as she moved to each,
and for just a moment, we were women
dreaming of an *Evening in Paris*.

Partial Eclipse

The year that "Ode to Billie Joe" wailed from A.M. radios,
and all of us 7th-grade girls whispered about what was thrown
from the bridge, our teacher brought us back to earth
with a celestial assignment. First, a film, projected
from a *clicking clacking* reel, starring the stages
of solar eclipse, a Moon meets Sun romance
so boring boys in the back of the room spent their time
carving obscenities into desks with box cutters borrowed
from the high school shop room. Breaking into groups,
we followed the purple mimeographed instructions, handouts
fragrant with duplicator fluid. We each took turns cutting
a rectangle into our boxes, donated by Ted's Market, then taped
foil over the aperture. Next, a pin prick in the silver center.
We taped a sheet of paper on the opposite end, a screen
for the eclipse peep show, then practiced placing the boxes
over our giggling heads, the teacher warning of blindness
if we looked directly at the Sun, and one boy muttered
that our eyeballs would boil. That morning in May,
just days before summer release, we gathered on the paved
play area, sectioned off for games of Four Square.
Turning our backs to the Sun, boxes placed over heads,
square like Halloween robots, we watched the small
projection, reversed image of the Sun, minus a cookie
bite corner. The experience lasted mere minutes, a let-down
after days of hype, but we did learn a lesson—to expect
disappointment if we were never allowed to stare directly,
if our lives were mere reflections, lived inside a camera obscura.

1970

Vietnam was still wrapping its jungle vines
around the young men unlucky enough
to win the draft lottery, except for the few
who found the money to enroll in college,
community or state, hoping to defer death.
Two years into high school, I learned
to be cool, wearing bell-bottom jeans
I embroidered with satin-stitched daisies
and peace signs, my ironed hair sweeping
the hip pockets. We wore black armbands
to protest, leather straps around foreheads
and legs, mimicking the cast of *Hair.*
And on weekends with nothing to do,
we dumped powdered washing detergent
into a local fountain, cheering the foam,
or sprayed *Flower Power* onto the press
box at the rodeo grounds, always something
that shouted, *Watch me! Watch me live!*

Unchained Melody

My father played *You Are My Sunshine* on guitar
and had my sister and me join him on the chorus,
while my mother only knew one song, *Clementine,*
whose words she taught us when we were small.
But I never sang in public, too shy to even look
another person in the eye. When our class sang
for Christmas programs, I could *In excelsis deo*
without fear because I was just one sheet-clad
angel in a band of many. But in high school choir,
when the teacher tested us for parts, he stopped,
wiped his glasses as if seeing me for the first time,
and said I should sing the lead in a song on variety
show night. When our quartet, clad in electric
blue satin blouses, took the stage, the bleachers
were still thumping, restless with those forced
to endure baton twirlers and lip-syncing eighth
graders in Beatles wigs, but when I took the mic,
crooned *Oh, my love, my darling,* the gymnasium
became as silent as an abandoned cathedral. I grew
stronger when the back-up joined, and for the first
time, I let the music flow, my melody unchained.

Shangri-La

At fourteen, I donned my black mini skirt
white button-up Oxford shirt, clip-on bow
tie, met up with my friend Donna, waiting
for the older boy who was to drive us, a boy
whose name has been lost to time. In his beater
Olds, we careened around curves to Shangri-La,
lake-side resort we could never have afforded
to enter if we had not been the hired help.
Inside the kitchen, the chef, a German man
who screamed in two languages, and his wife,
Inge, pushed us toward the salad station,
the warming bins for dinner rolls, barked
out instructions that filled my head like steam.
My main job was bus girl, standing statuesque
with a thirty-pound metal tray of filet mignon
as the waitress chatted and cooed for tips,
lifting off the dishes slowly and placing
them with flourish, while my arms grew
numb. At the end of the night, when tips
were split, my waitress, squat woman, bitter-
eyed, pushed a dollar bill and two quarters
across the table top, daring me to defy her.
I slipped the money into my fringed purse,
resolved never to be in her crepe-soled shoes.

Motown Comes to Notown

Even if our older friends' cars—retired hearse with top
sparkling like gold lame' or '52 Chevy named the Gray
Greaser—could have survived the thirteen-hour drive
to Detroit, we were too young to make our way
up to Motown, so it had to come down to us.
In '65, we watched in black and white as Smokey
Robinson performed with the Miracles on *Hullabaloo,*
surrounded by cages containing dancers in fringed
dresses that shook when they shimmied, others boot
clad as they crowded around the singer, frantic
in the frug, the mashed potato, the swim, the pony.
And in '67, we still played his hit each Friday
night at the V.F.W. hall, where the junior high
boys lined the walls like carnival milk bottles.
But one, Ronnie, who divided his time between
Vegas and the Ozark foothills, came clad
in a blue silk shirt with ballooning sleeves,
and when someone dropped the needle
onto a 45 of Mr. Robinson belting *Going
to a Go-Go,* Ronnie took to the floor,
held a mock mic, slid across the wooden
slats, smoothed by a hundred years of shuffle,
and brought Motown to our little Notown, Oklahoma.

Ode to the Gray Greaser

O, Gray Greaser, with your push button
starter and old person smell, you who
wheeled out brand spanking new three years
before I was born—'52 Chevy with curved
lines and striped seats—I remember you
fondly. You, Gray Greaser, sped up
and down Main, radio blaring a local
rock channel that must have disturbed
your automotive senses, obviously
a Perry Como kind of guy. Around
and around, a conveyor belt of teen-
age hormones, you glided through
drive-in parking lots, allowed long-
haired boys to lean against windows
or lounge on your hood like hoods.
O, Gray Greaser, you never asked
for much in return, just a little fuel
that we pumped from the DX,
a dollar at a time. I hope someone
found you, after my never-to-be
bother-in-law wrecked you. I hope
you were rescued, now sitting, shiny,
at a car show, your grille grinning.

Persephone's Seduction

How did he approach her as she sowed dreams in her garden?
Perhaps he neared gently, clothed in a garment sewn to hide
his true nature. Maybe he even hummed a bee melody, asked
her to dance, took her hands, delicate as Luna moths, twirled
her amid the feathered ferns, their fronds swirled like conch.
And maybe he spoke words that one so young had never heard
before—declarations of her beauty, his desire to know her soul.
Perhaps she fell for the nectar-laced words falling from his lips
for one second too long before she felt his arms web around
her, haul her screaming to his Hadean chariot, waiting to whisk
her into an eternal Underworld where he claimed kinghood.

How did he approach her as she stood against the wall of a dance
hall upstairs from an abandoned grocery? Perhaps he neared
with swagger, fresh from his stint in Vietnam, dressed in blue
velvet vest the color of a robin's eggs, not really asking
but holding out a hand and jerking her to the wooden floor,
as the Hollies spun out "She Was a Long Cool Woman,"
while she was none of these, aside from wearing a sateen
dress that whirled around her legs, an ebony wheel of fabric.
Maybe she was too shy to refuse as he pulled her down the stairs
to his pitch black '69 Chevelle, trimmed with white racing stripes,
roaring its way to a hundred, as he reveled in her virginal screams.

Outside the Snak Shak—1972

She stands outside the Snak Shak
wearing cut-off Levis, fringed
hems too short, along with a tube
top, covered by lace bolero. Cher
hair shimmers to her waist
as she places bare feet on the seat
of a wooden picnic table, eases
herself onto the top, just as two
cars crunch the gravel—one powder
blue '62 Impala, borrowed
from his grandmother, the other
a black SS Super Sport with wide
white stripes, a gift to himself
for surviving Nam. She knows
them both, knows that each wants her
to make a choice, so they idle
and wait, while she breaks the shell
of her double dip cone that even then
tastes a lot like regret.

Persephone's Seduction

How did he approach her as she sowed dreams in her garden?
Perhaps he neared gently, clothed in a garment sewn to hide
his true nature. Maybe he even hummed a bee melody, asked
her to dance, took her hands, delicate as Luna moths, twirled
her amid the feathered ferns, their fronds swirled like conch.
And maybe he spoke words that one so young had never heard
before—declarations of her beauty, his desire to know her soul.
Perhaps she fell for the nectar-laced words falling from his lips
for one second too long before she felt his arms web around
her, haul her screaming to his Hadean chariot, waiting to whisk
her into an eternal Underworld where he claimed kinghood.

How did he approach her as she stood against the wall of a dance
hall upstairs from an abandoned grocery? Perhaps he neared
with swagger, fresh from his stint in Vietnam, dressed in blue
velvet vest the color of a robin's eggs, not really asking
but holding out a hand and jerking her to the wooden floor,
as the Hollies spun out "She Was a Long Cool Woman,"
while she was none of these, aside from wearing a sateen
dress that whirled around her legs, an ebony wheel of fabric.
Maybe she was too shy to refuse as he pulled her down the stairs
to his pitch black '69 Chevelle, trimmed with white racing stripes,
roaring its way to a hundred, as he reveled in her virginal screams.

Outside the Snak Shak—1972

She stands outside the Snak Shak
wearing cut-off Levis, fringed
hems too short, along with a tube
top, covered by lace bolero. Cher
hair shimmers to her waist
as she places bare feet on the seat
of a wooden picnic table, eases
herself onto the top, just as two
cars crunch the gravel—one powder
blue '62 Impala, borrowed
from his grandmother, the other
a black SS Super Sport with wide
white stripes, a gift to himself
for surviving Nam. She knows
them both, knows that each wants her
to make a choice, so they idle
and wait, while she breaks the shell
of her double dip cone that even then
tastes a lot like regret.

If Life Were a Rom-Com

that seven-year-old girl who gnaws
on the ends of her Pippi Longstocking
braids as she suffers the bus ride
to school each morning, blushing
vermillion as he, golden football god,
takes two steps at a time, swaggers past
the driver with greeting, before meeting
the top of her head with his palm, a pat
of affection as he calls her *Cutie,* heads
to the back with the big kids, that girl

would bloom into a black-haired beauty
sporting mini-skirt and fringed suede jacket
as she heads to his house to babysit—four
children only five years after graduation
and his wedding to a pageant queen from two
towns over—and the girl would try not meet his eye
as he hands her the buck twenty-five an hour,
asks her how school is going, offers tutoring
in history, his favorite subject, if she needs it,
and she would say thanks, vow not to see him alone

until five years and one divorce later, she slips
dimes into a washer at the laundromat, soaking
in her own failure, when he appears beside her,
still handsome and tanned from building houses,
running cattle, and he says that he's heard
about her split, confides that he and his wife
have called it quits, and yes, it is hard on the kids
but harder still for them to hear the constant
barrage of bitter accusations, declarations
of regret that come with marrying too young,

and she would agree to meet him after work on Friday,
to go for a ride to talk, to see him again the next
week, take in a show, dine in the finest restaurants
in the tri-state, hold his hands, sandpapered
with labor, to finally feel the warmth of his kiss—
so many fairy tale years in the making—until
one day, a woman she barely knows, approaches
her with hand on hip, asks if she knows the man
she is dating is married, merely separated, soon
to be reconciled with his wife, and that girl

would never see him again until nearly fifty years
have passed, when inside the cafeteria, where alums
gather for a banquet, he seeks her out, whispers,
asks if he can talk to her, says he is sorry for all
he did, sorry that he was in such a dark place,
sorry for any deception, sorry that he let her
get away, declares that he has thought of her
his entire life, will never stop thinking of her,
and if life were a rom-com, that girl, no longer
a girl, would kiss his lips to silence—but it's not.

PART III

*Home is one's birthplace,
ratified by memory.*
—Henry Grumwald

Education of a Sixth-Generation Cherokee Refugee

My grandmother never taught me
how to cut the finest honeysuckle
vines or river cane, how to soak
until pliable enough to reliably
weave baskets dyed from blood
root, sassafras, walnut bark.

My grandmother never taught me
to plant three sisters—corn, beans,
squash. She never showed me
how to predict weather with persimmon
seeds. Or how to make kanuchi—
gathering hickory nuts still inside
hulls, cracking, sifting, mashing with pestle.

My grandmother never taught me
how to dig the native red clay, to coil
the strips, to carve a wooden paddle
for imprinting pots, fired with White Oak.

My grandmother never taught me
the Green Corn Dance or the Myth
of the Milky Way or how to read
Sequoyah's symbols.

My grandmother only taught me fear—
to avoid rocking an empty chair, never
to lay a coat across the foot of a bed,
to toss salt over my shoulder if I spilled
the shaker, to spit into the road if a black

cat crossed, to recognize death in the daytime visitation of an owl or in the nighttime dream of a white horse, the same one that had come to her, knelt, carried away her own mother.

Even in Oklahoma

We sat in our third-grade desks, sharing aloud
the *Weekly Reader,* propaganda rag, touting
the tale, complete with smiling caricatures
of prim Pilgrims and white-washed Natives,
shaking hands before sharing a meal
of Butterball turkey and perfectly crimped
pumpkin pies, with a caption crowing
about the generosity of Indians who kept
their new friends alive by showing them
how to bury fish beside the corn kernels,
how rot gives way to life, how something
must die so something new grows, never
once mentioning what the white people
brought to the Indians, what they took
away, and although we students were sprouted
from seeds of tribes driven to this land
from ancestral homes, not once did the teacher
mention the white tide that washed upon our soil,
swept us along the Trail that brought us
here to this place, where we traced
our fingers onto vanilla paper, colored
a headdress on a cartoon elder.

The Land of Milk and Honey

The same year Steinbeck gave birth to the Joads,
my father, only nine years old at the time, rode
in the back seat of his family's '36 Plymouth sedan
with its Mayflower ship hood ornament, symbol
of all the places a driver could go, the adventures
awaiting. Purchased when lead and zinc miners
in the Ozark foothills were still lifting buckets
of prosperity from the pits, the car was the only
thing they owned when the owners shackled
the gates. They tied feather-stuffed ticking
to the top, crammed tins and jars into the trunk,
and hit Route 66, west to California. Oranges
that they only saw at Christmas time hung
from trees, free for the picking, they heard.
The sun shone every day, but still, some way,
the fruit sipped sweet water from the ground.
But the car over-heated near Needles, last stop
before crossing desert, and gas station owners
frowned on Okie invaders. Motor wheezing,
at last they found fields and orchards, hordes
of workers bending and climbing. Peaches
were ripening, sending their scent floating,
so my father's father and older brother Harley
were hired, warned they would not be paid
for bruised fruit. For weeks, they slept in musty
tents, until they heard of an abandoned house, no
doors or windows but a real roof. And one
day, when my father was exploring the yard,
he heard a humming coming from the ground,
a noise so loud he feared a quake. His father,
just arriving home, took the boy by the hand,

and he led him to the spot. Smiling, his father
raised a hollow log, and a host of bees took flight,
threatened, as he held the wood high, crashed
it against the ground, came away with comb
dripping, so much sweetness he felt no sting.

Uncle Rocky

killed a man once, or at least tried,
slitting his throat out of fear when the owner
caught Rocky robbing his rabbit hutches.
The knife, meant to still squealing throats of fur,
drew across the old man's neck when he drew
a gun, shouted to stop, moved too slowly.
It was a time when lines of washed-out,
washed-up men stood waiting for hand-outs
that never lasted until the next doling.
It was a time when the whole world
was faded like denim run through lye
too many times and dried on a drooping
line. Rocky was not a bad man—one prone
to breaking into random harmonica tunes
or stroking the mane of his ebony plow
horse—but hunger is a feral dog, baring
its teeth, forgetting it was ever tamed.

Grand Lake O' the Cherokees

Men left their farms, joined the CCC, swallowed
their Okie pride, cashed their government checks,
telling themselves they were constructing a future
for their progeny—too many to survive on farms
of two-hundred-acre hard scrabble plots plowed
out of limestone. When the dam was completed,
the gates switched open, the Grand River gushed
into the valleys, pushed over persimmon and pawpaw
trees in its rush. This verdant land had been allotted
to the Cherokees, children and grandchildren,
of those who walked from the South, mouths dry
and silent with loss. But even here the government
took back their promise, forced a few dollars
into Indian pockets, and gave the lake their name.
My second great-grandmother, widowed by bandits,
bitten by a copperhead at eighty-five, continued
to roam the hills, plucking dew berries like garnet
pendants, until she was forced to gather remnants
of her life, hitch her skirts, and scurry to a nearby
town while the waters drowned the memories
made inside her house, hewn from old growth
timber. The oak dining table floated to the ceiling,
all six chairs still tucked beneath as if waiting
for the dinner bell, the pushing back, scraping
of wood on wood, the murmur of hurried grace.

Saturday Night Refuge

Here's to all the men from my childhood
who gathered inside living rooms of shotgun
houses, walls plastered with wallpaper hung
fast with flour and water paste.

Men who spent their days inside the night
of lead and zinc mines—digging, dragging,
dynamiting—carrying the dust of their drudgery
inside black lungs.

Men who toiled at the tire plant, feet planted
in one spot, sweat seeping through socks, eating
away at the leather of crepe-soled shoes
as they inhaled carbon black, dipped hands
into benzene, felt their backs bend like rubber.

Men who walked behind the plow horse, tilling
the gardens of widows for a few dollars a day,
paid little for their time because they had done
time—set a barn on fire, slit a neighbor's throat.

Men who made little money except for other men,
whose names emblazoned brick buildings.

But on Saturday nights, they took some refuge
in hand-rolled cigarettes, strong tugs on a bottle
of stronger whiskey, a game or two of Pitch
or Dominos, and the bittersweet harmonies
of a Guthrie song, strummed on a pawnshop
Stella guitar, backed by a mouth harp's twang,
that whined out the simple unfairness of it all.

Made in America

My father was one of the men who,
coming back, shed his Army uniform,
traded his sniper rifle for textbooks,
meaning to milk the G.I. bill for a monthly
check as he sat in junior college classes,
surrounded by teenage girls drawing hearts
across their notebooks, writing *Elvis, Marlon,
or Tab* inside. He did not mean to fall in love
with learning, which only made the break-up
of graduation harder, when he had to face
his fate—a man with a family needed the factory
pay. For thirty years he donned his navy blue
pocket tees and crepe-soled shoes, carried his lunch
bucket, shaped like a black metal barn. He chewed
Beechnut as he lifted, pulled, cut—creating tires
on an assembly line. In summer, when temperatures
blazed, he popped salt tablets that turned his sweat
white. And every few years, he walked the picket
lines during strikes to demand a quarter raise. Stench
of rubber resided inside his nose, and he did not know
as he dipped his fingers into benzene or wiped carbon
black away with his hanky that he was holding
his own death in his hands, as he numbed his mind,
toiled away, night after night on the graveyard shift.

The Hands She Was Dealt

My mother thought she had been dealt
the king of hearts when my father, wearing
his pleated Carey Grant pants and glossy
black boots sauntered into Woolworth's,
scoped out the merchandise, and headed
toward the candy counter, moat of glass,
enclosing heaped red hots and chocolate
kisses. Ruby, his cousin who worked
the sock department, keeping the pairs
matched and folded, had arranged
for him to purchase a pack of Juicy Fruit,
and if he liked my mother's smile, red
lips blooming with Helena Rubinstein's
Bed of Roses, he was to introduce himself,
suggest a Coke at the lunch counter. Mother's
hands, nails trimmed and unpolished—dime
store regulation—must have shaken, counting
back his change. And when she took his hand
eleven months later, she thought her farmgirl
days, left behind after high school graduation,
were a dusty memory, traded for Loretta
Young dresses and fancy Jell-O molds, not
knowing his dream was to leave the town,
own a few acres, her life thrown in reverse.
For thirty years, she dropped seeds into holes,
turned potato eyes down, picked beans and peas,
flicked worms from tomato leaves, gathered
clutches of warm eggs from nests, twisted
chickens' necks when they were too old
to lay, pinched their singed pin feathers,
her fingers plucking them like mournful harp strings.

My Mother Said Nothing

My mother said nothing when Gus, old Army
buddy of my father's, came tornadoing through
town—blonde and bronze like Tod Stiles,
a.k.a. Martin Milner, speeding down Rt. 66
in his Horizon Blue Corvette convertible.

My mother said nothing when he pulled
my father away from Sunday pot roast
to try out his speed boat on Grand Lake
with friends she had never met,
names she would never know.

My mother said nothing when they spent
all day on water skis, draining cans
of Coors from a cooler, coming home
long after dark, arms draped around
each other like stumbling scarecrows.

My mother said nothing when blisters
formed on my father's back, blazing
suns she tried to extinguish with cool
cloths, baking soda, compresses
of cold, clotted oatmeal.

My mother said nothing when Monday
came, Tuesday, and still he could not
work, could not wear a shirt. Silence
as she sat beside his prone body,
peeling away his layers with vicious
tenderness.

Johnny Keene

Waiting inside our blue and white Ford Galaxie,
my mother locked the doors just in time.
Down the street came Johnny Keene, cousin
to my father but rarely claimed. He lapped
one long leg in front of the other, like a squirrel
tight-roping a telephone wire. Talking to air,
he twisted his head, whirled as if fly-bitten,
before spotting us. Too slow with the crank
windows, we shrank away as he leaned
inside. *They're after me again.*
Before we could ask who,
F.B.I., C.I.A., Russians, he whispered.
How beautiful he looked just then,
his sleek hair ruffled crow-like,
his eyes so black and wide
they held a raven's wings.
No one's after you, Johnny Keene.
Confused, he pulled back,
walked away with rounded shoulders.
Inside the car, silence replaced the madness,
and the beauty.

When PBS Came to Picher, Oklahoma

Each week, my father and his friends gathered
at the pool hall, or what *had been* a pool hall,
the length of Main Street now full of buildings—
boarded or burned out—that had been something,
sometime before the government declared the town
a disaster, due to its metal-clad water and cave-ins,
just waiting to inhale the houses—shotgun
row homes with a covered stoop, one window.
When mines and bombs were booming,
Picher pumped out half the lead and zinc
the Doughboys needed to beat the Huns
so they could come home and die of the Spanish
flu or spend their lives trying to forget the shell-
shocked trenches.

Eighty years after Armistice, my father's group
met at the abandoned building to play bluegrass
and gospel each Sunday afternoon, while remnants
of the mines—looming misplaced mountains of chat—
acted as backdrop. And once, some young people,
armed with cameras and microphones, tracked
the lonesome harmony to find the men, dressed
in their Sunday best—plaid shirts tucked into tooled
belts with their names engraved across the back,
while in front, silver buckles glinted with calf ropers
or long-horn steers. The strangers were shooting
a film about the town—what it had been, had become.

My father told stories, how before there were unions,
miners were lowered into shafts inside rusty buckets,
held by questionable cables, how they had no masks

to protect their lungs, only a kerchief to slow the killing
dust that they dragged inside the pits, how even the mules,
blind from years of darkness, were left to perish
underground when the mines shut down. He showed
them a photograph—still framed on the wall—of a crew
posed at the mouth of a mine, their faces smudged,
hands beyond cleaning. He pointed out
his father, dead at forty-five,
his brother, gone at forty-two,
Uncle Rocky, lost inside a bottle his whole life.

When one young man asked to record a song,
the old musicians took up their Gibson mandolins
and Martin guitars, and while my father sang lead
on "Precious Memories," his friend Kenny
harmonized with his high twang. The camera
crew filmed, had them sign releases, then packed
their gear with promise of making them proud.
But when the show aired, the whole scene was gone,
the song cut, the men's words lost to time
restraints.

Now, decades later, Picher is a ghost town,
and the men themselves are spirits, haunting
the pool hall, lifting their voices in praise
to the Lord or some girl named Liza Jane,
still waiting for their solitary brush with fame.

Remembering Oklahoma

I recall the hoofbeat syllables of Sallisaw. Seminole. Sapulpa.
The drumming of Tahlequah. Tonkawa. Tecumseh.
Gaze out on the rolling Neosho River, heavy with downed
trees and spoonbill. Hear the echoes of names being called
through time: Wilma Jean, Jimmy Ray, Sammy Dale. Savor
fried okra, fry bread, boiled cabbage with bacon drippings.

I am brought back to red dirt roads, smelling of August
rain. Route 66 with crumbling motels, staring with blank
windows. Scattered chat piles, corpses of lead and zinc mines.
I feel the wind that carries the remnants of Woody Guthrie
and Gene Autry tunes. The same wind that churns and whirls
above storm cellars filled with canned peaches and prayers.

I go back to lilacs. Pastures of Indian paint brush. Pawpaws
and persimmons. Scissor-tailed swallows swooping
through skeletal barns. I am transported to a family farm
where Biblical cedars keep sentry, where a sulphur spring
bubbles up through sandstone, where the apricot tree grows
tiny moons, where the killdeer, dragging its wing, leads me away.

PART IV

Unless we remember, we cannot understand.
—E. M. Forster

Chambers of the Heart

As a small child, he sat for hours
with the oversized book
on his undersized lap—
a tome about the human body—
its illustrations of man, sans
skin, his tendons twisted
in colors like electrical wire,
the femur and ulna, ball and
socket, the inset 3D plastic
model of the heart—hinged
to reveal the atria and ventricles—
the close-up of a face—one side
handsome as a magazine model,
the other a skull sporting a blue eye
afloat in its hollow—his teeth caught
in a death grin. We smiled
and concurred, *Doctor. Surgeon.*
Now, one step from manhood,
he spends hours with his arms
wrapped around the body
of his Martin, suturing notes
and words together, singing
about the chambers of the heart
that he is just learning to open.

Trespassers

When heat waves wash over summer lawns
and streets, the boys first appear—three,
sometimes four—sailing on their bikes, arms
raised upright, balancing with knobby knees,
or abandoning the banana seats—peeling from glide
of shorts on vinyl—to stand as if catching breezes
on a ship's bow. They never use their kick stands,
silver wands snapped in place, instead dropping
the bikes—wheels still spinning—onto an empty
lot, lush in Bermuda. For hours, the buccaneers
anchor beneath evergreen trees that mark town
from farm. The ruffians chuck pine cone cannon balls
at each other or search through yard debris—secretly
dumped by a thoughtless neighbor—seeking out sticks
straight and sharp enough to morph into swords.
They pull up chunks of asphalt, ragged where street
meets the bed of brown needles, stockpiling a brigand's
bounty. Sticky trunks, split down the middle by August
storms, form gang planks they force the smallest to walk.
This crew should be banished, sent home to safety,
but the light is already growing slant, the days shorter,
and everyone knows that pirates always die young.

The Reason We Gather for the Solar Eclipse

It is not because the light pinholes through oak
leaves, creating a circus of crescent suns
upon the lawn—performers in spangled costumes.

It is not to feel the day lose its way,
the waning of warmth sending icy
fingers to stroke our prickled arms.

It is not to see the scenery's color seeping
away to sepia, like a tin-type photograph
of unremembered ancestors.

It is not hearing the sudden hush
of songbirds rushing to roost
among the limbs of shadowed pines.

It is not observing orb-weaving spiders
dismantling their webs, stowing them
like returned sailors' rigging.

It is not to keep a date with Venus,
spreading her goddess glow, outshining
the stars, startled by their daytime awakening.

It is not to share the wealth of Bailey's
beads, strung around the Moon or the golden
corona crowning the royal Sun.

No, we gather for that moment, after totality's
darkness, when we stand, faces upturned,
waiting for that brilliant flash of promise,

and we think, *Ah, yes, this is the way it will be.*

Mesa Verde

Inspired by Robert Frost's A Cliff Dwelling

No golden sky the day a pair
of Quaker cowboys, yet still green
from Kansas plains, bent low their heads
against the snow, seeking out signs
of errant hooves gone astray, reigned
on the edge of a canyon rim.

Through the flakes, traces of towers
and walls rose up, a cliff dwelling
like some primeval palace. Down
they rode, then stopped. With lariats
and tree trunk, they fashioned a way
up the walls of sandstone and shale
where others used to climb and crawl.

Inside the honeycomb of rooms,
the dust of oh so many years
ago rose up and settled down,
and all around it was as if
the ones who once resided here
had simply walked away and left
behind the remnants of a life—

woven turkey feather robes, bows
and arrows, baskets brim with corn.
Upon the walls the drovers found
the pictures one had drawn or carved—
his world of birds and bighorn sheep—

and all around, a human hand
first dipped in paint then pressed to print
so those who came might not forget
the disappearing last of him.*

* This line was lifted from Frost's *A Cliff Dwelling*.

POW

Relic of the first forgotten war,
he passes by our house each day,
riding the remnants of a bike with wire
baskets, one on each side. Dodging
cars behind him, a rangy black dog
presses nose to asphalt. From time
to time, the man stops, pokes weeds
with a stick, as if searching for lost land mines,
uncovering, instead, Coke cans, beer bottles.
Talking, smiling, he empties rain water
and pockets the spoils. Warmer weather,
he wears the same brown coat, Goodwill
castoff from a larger man's suit. Winter,
he sports a green army jacket and cap
with flaps like the flying aces wore.
He lives alone inside a burned-out shell,
and when planes fly low, humming,
droning giant wasps dusting crops,
he shoulders his rifle, marches into the field,
and returns fire. Just once he gets lucky,
a direct hit. One bullet slices through the skin
of the cockpit. Later that afternoon,
the sheriffs' cars surround the hollow
fortification, while a TV station's helicopter
hovers, the crew itself shooting, as the old
soldier is cuffed, still a prisoner of war.

Claude

Wheat threshing time in Indiana, my Uncle Mac,
on furlough from Fort Monroe, Virginia, would
sit in his showroom Mercury, feet on the dash
where a little rubber-bladed fan was mounted,
while I, sweating, loaded and unloaded bundles
of wheat. He'd holler, *Every day in the Army
is just like Sunday on a farm.* So I enlisted
in August of '39, no notion of happenings
an ocean away. Arriving in the Philippines
in 1941, I was named wire chief. Sleeping
on a cot just outside the switchboard room,
General MacArthur shook me hard, shook me
to the core with *Japan just bombed Pearl Harbor.*

We moved command to Malinta Tunnel
while the parade ground cratered around us.
I spied Bataan through the spotting scopes—
howitzers, big guns all lined up, on their own
death march. We ran the white flag
up the pole, set fire to the switchboard.
Captured, we suffered in the bottom deck
of a freighter, landing on Thanksgiving Day.
Soldiers taught us to count off in Japanese,
fed us rice with watery soup. Skeletons
with shovels, we dug a dry dock, grave
days, believing in nothing but the B29's,
their vapor trails writing letters from home.

In '44, I barely weighed a hundred, no more,
when I was transported to Osaka #5 Camp.
The prisoners unloaded salt, leather, cast
iron, and my savior—soybeans, beads

of gold—rationed three times a day.
Firebombing started in July, burning
the building where we lived. The brick
factory became our home until we heard
of a terrible weapon that had wiped away
a city, soon a second one. Reborn by death,
we passed through the gates, and guards
racked their rifles, let us go. People ask
how I survived. They always want to know.

When I was boy, trapping foxes on the farm,
I came across my father's ewe, caught,
wild-eyed, steel jaws vising her front foot.
I freed her, boosted her up, walked her back
to the barn. In the morning, she was dead,
not from injury, but from the snare of lost
hope, surrendering to the enemy within.

Horsman

The inn-keeper tells me that after the war,
he was never truly afraid, not even
during those years when he and Blossom, a shepherd mix,
traveled the backroads in his rusty Ford LTD,
spending nights at rest areas or roadside parks,
where they pitched a plastic tarp over ropes
hung from tree limbs, before sharing a beef jerky
breakfast and heading out to search for treasures
in dim shops and dusty garages, ferreting
random pieces of china or silver that he struck
from the list.

And before that, when he hitched a ride
to Sarasota, joining the Royal Hanneford Circus,
pitching in to raise the tents, winds sometimes roaring
across the grounds, flapping the canvas
until it snapped like a whip, he was never afraid.
Nor did he fear the animals—
majestic Lippizzaner stallions with hooves of steel,
white tigers swiping away the trainer's crop,
elephants with their wise resentment.

After the war, he was never truly afraid
except at one place—the Horsman Doll Factory—
where he mixed the plastics to be poured,
formed into dolls. All around, their eyes,
waiting transplant, rolled inside trays,
while stacks of arms, legs, heads—
pre-capitated, brought to mind a time

he'd long ago tried to forget, especially
when the workers pulled new babies
out of the molds, and each let loose
one long, horrifying squeal.

Disappeared

*One academic researcher contends that as many as 40,000 children
may have died in or because of their poor care at U.S.-run schools.*
—Reuters

Come, find where they buried me
beneath a land not my own.
A place of pain, where men in collars
used Christ's suffering to justify mine,
strapping me with cat-o-nine tails,
forcing me to bear the cross for a God
who did not wear my skin,
who did not live in ancient tree or rock.

A place where women wearing wings
on their heads married Jesus and adopted
us children, born of sin, punished
for our parents' desires, for our own.
Slaps across the face or lashes for using
our native tongue—dark confinement
for days if those words were a prayer.
A place where our memories were stolen.

A place where we were scalded with kerosene,
where our hair was shamed and sheared.
If caught running away, we suffered the razor,
heads shaved—girls and boys—because they knew
our spirit lived there, blowing free in the wind.
A place where we swallowed the secrets
they swore us to, buried them deep
where they could not haunt us or them.

A place where we, too, were buried
in coffins hammered by classmates, disappeared
in unmarked graves dug by our brothers.
Come, find where they buried me.
Bind my bones in braided sweetgrass,
cradle me next to your breast,
give me a name that means *Justice,*
and sing me home to my people.

The Poetry of Their Names

> ... the National Crime Information Center cited 5,712 reports of slain or missing Native American women and girls in 2016... but only 116 of those were logged into a Department of Justice database.
> —CNN

This is Crow Nation, a couple miles from Custer
Battlefield, where the general, clad in buckskins,
his newly-trimmed curls shawling his ears,
met his match—payback for massacres
his men committed, deeds not committed
to history books today. Two little girls sit
beside a folding table, the sun catching
their hair like blackbird feathers.
They are selling jewelry, not chunky
turquoise squash blossoms or silver
conchos, but tiny beads, strung together
by a child's hands. These girls, no older
than eight or nine, are alone on this dusty
road. A pup tent, the kind you might find
at a backyard sleep-over, squats nearby.
Is it a refuge from heat, or do they sleep
here, cradled against each other?
One smiles, eyes downcast, points out
the pieces she has made, and I make
a show of selecting just the right bracelets
I will never wear. Where is their mother?
Has she not heard of the vanishing
of Native girls? Has she not seen
the lists, photos so similar to these two
sisters? Those girls also trusted too much,
and not even the poetry of their names—
Brightwings, Stands on a Cloud, Not Afraid—
could save them.

A place where we, too, were buried
in coffins hammered by classmates, disappeared
in unmarked graves dug by our brothers.
Come, find where they buried me.
Bind my bones in braided sweetgrass,
cradle me next to your breast,
give me a name that means *Justice,*
and sing me home to my people.

The Poetry of Their Names

> . . . the National Crime Information Center cited 5,712 reports of slain or missing Native American women and girls in 2016 . . . but only 116 of those were logged into a Department of Justice database.
> —CNN

This is Crow Nation, a couple miles from Custer
Battlefield, where the general, clad in buckskins,
his newly-trimmed curls shawling his ears,
met his match—payback for massacres
his men committed, deeds not committed
to history books today. Two little girls sit
beside a folding table, the sun catching
their hair like blackbird feathers.
They are selling jewelry, not chunky
turquoise squash blossoms or silver
conchos, but tiny beads, strung together
by a child's hands. These girls, no older
than eight or nine, are alone on this dusty
road. A pup tent, the kind you might find
at a backyard sleep-over, squats nearby.
Is it a refuge from heat, or do they sleep
here, cradled against each other?
One smiles, eyes downcast, points out
the pieces she has made, and I make
a show of selecting just the right bracelets
I will never wear. Where is their mother?
Has she not heard of the vanishing
of Native girls? Has she not seen
the lists, photos so similar to these two
sisters? Those girls also trusted too much,
and not even the poetry of their names—
Brightwings, Stands on a Cloud, Not Afraid—
could save them.

Medicare Physical

Our family doctor makes notes on a printout,
asking you the difficult questions we try to tell
ourselves we will never need an answer to.
If you collapse in the office,
should we perform life-saving measures?
If your heart stops beating,
should we shock you back to life?
If you need a feeding tube temporarily,
should we insert one?
Each time, we chime a *yes* in unison.
The decision, in the end, will be mine,
though. I know the weight of your life
will be a heavy burden to carry. Arriving
home, we sit in the car a few moments,
and you recall the winter morning, twenty
years ago, when you hurried to your truck,
late as usual for the college students brave
enough to face the eight o'clock cold.
Your breath left contrails as you slid
onto your crackling leather seats, fired up
the engine. The sound is one now gouged
into your memory. A stray kitten, no doubt
dumped the night before, had taken refuge
beneath your hood. It was still alive, mangled
beyond repair, and you could not bear
to hear the wailing, the cries that never stopped
until you found a concrete block. The hardest
thing you ever did, you say, was to be kind.

An Apology to My Father

After reading "On Loved Ones Telling the Dying To 'Let Go'"
by Reeves Keyworth

In my defense, it was a hospice nurse, the same
one who instructed us to look for dappling,
mottled ankles, the rattled breathing, who
suggested that the best a loved one can do
is to give the dying permission to depart.

Now I think I should have channeled Dylan
Thomas, told you to rage against the night.
Or maybe I should have held your hand
as you leapt through your *delirium of memory*—
you and Uncle Harley slogging through snow
with bats, bashing rabbits for family food,
furs stretched to dry for trade. Or you

and the neighborhood boys, easily mistaken
for The Little Rascals, swiping summer melons
from nearby gardens, stealing tarnished pennies
from a cemetery statue of a Quapaw chief,
his hands open for the offerings you prayed
were not cursed. Maybe you relived memories

of all the other near-death brushes—nearly
drowning at five when an older cousin thought
a swimming lesson was a toss into the deepest
pool at Tar Creek. Or maybe you remembered
the time at twelve, while climbing a mining
scaffold, you swung out over a pit with pitch
for a bottom, holding on to the rusted arm
meant to hoist buckets of men, whose ghosts
gave the other boys strength to pull you,

screaming, back from the blackness. Or maybe
memories at death are gentle ones—singing
hymns on Sunday morning, stroking the head
of a stray calico, wiping an apricot with shirttail
before biting sweetness surrounding stone.

Perhaps there are no visual memories at all—
just the touch of lips and hands. And maybe
you could not hear the words I want to take
back now, but could only feel my fingers,
pressed against your bare chest, the warmth
as they searched for those last precious beats.

Dreams Deferred

Those last days in a nursing home, rehabbing
from a long hospital stay, my father gathered
in the rec room with the other residents,
and I thought he would enjoy the surprise
when the members of his bluegrass band,
the one he had picked with for benefits
and Sunday socials, showed up to play.
But as they harmonized on old hymns,
the ones he always sang lead on, he mouthed
the words, voice no longer strong enough
to be heard. He could not quell the tears
that caught in his whiskers, and he whispered,
No more before I wheeled him back down
the hall to his death bed. He dreamt of playing
at the Opry, wearing suits with sequins sewn
in wagon wheel designs. He dreamt of taking
bows in concert halls, of autographing slick
programs. He dreamt of hearing his songs
on the radio or on juke boxes in Route 66
taverns. He dreamt that he would be a star,
remembered like Hank Williams, but life
nudged him away from his musical dreams,
like a determined dog that shoves its head
under a hand, demanding attention. Deferred
too long, his dreams died of thirst. I only wish
that he could have died first.

About the Author

Linda Neal Reising, a native of Oklahoma and citizen of the Cherokee Nation, has been published in numerous journals, including *The Southern Indiana Review, The Comstock Review,* and *Nimrod*. Her work has also appeared in a number of anthologies, including *Fruitflesh: Seeds of Inspiration for Women Who Write* (HarperCollins), *And Know This Place: Poetry of Indiana* (Indiana Historical Society Press), and *Let Me Say This: A Dolly Parton Poetry Anthology* (Madville Press).

She was named the winner of the 2012 Writer's Digest Poetry Competition, and her poetry has been nominated for a Pushcart Prize four times. She was also named the 2024 Official Eclipse Poet of Indiana by Indiana Humanities.

Her first chapbook, *Re-Writing Family History* (Finishing Line Press), was a finalist for the 2015 Oklahoma Book Award and winner of the Oklahoma Writing Federation Poetry Book Contest. Reising's first full-length collection, *The Keeping* (Finishing Line Press), won the 2020 Kops-Fetherling Phoenix Award for Outstanding New Voice in Poetry.

Her second, *Stone Roses* (Kelsay Books, 2021), was a finalist for the Oklahoma Book Award and the WILLA Award, as well as winning the 2022 Eric Hoffer Award and the Western Heritage Wrangler Award. *VIVIA ~ The Legend of Vivia Thomas: A Novelette in Poems* (Kelsay Books, 2023), her latest full-length book, was a finalist for the 2024 Oklahoma Book Award, the International Book Award, and the Person of the Year Book Award. It was named a winner in the Bookfest Awards, the Feathered Quill Book Awards, the Typesmith Book Awards, the Human Relations Adventure Poetry Prize Director's Choice, and the Literary Global Book Awards for Poetry and Novelette.

Reising's chapbook *Perpetual Astonishment,* won the Beyond Words Chapbook Award 2023 and was published in 2024. Her first book of fiction, *Cigar Box of Loss: Stories from Route 66,* is forthcoming from Belle Point Press.

Email: lv2write@tds.net
Website: lindanealreising.weebly.com
Facebook: Linda Neal Reising
Instagram: @nealreising

www.ingramcontent.com/pod-product-compliance
Lightning Source LLC
Chambersburg PA
CBHW031202160426
43193CB00008B/471